The Ongoing Struggle
Volume 3

RED SEAS
Overcoming

BRENDA S. JACKSON, PH.D.

*Priority*ON!
p u b l i c a t i o n

D1333882

*Priority*ONE Publications
P. O. Box 34722 / Detroit, MI 48234
E-mail: info@priorityonebooks.com
URL: http://www.priorityonebooks.com
1 (313) 312-5318

ISBN 13:   978-1-933972-44-2
ISBN 10:   1-933972-44-0

Edited by Patricia A. Hicks
Cover and interior design by PriorityON[E]

TABLE OF CONTENTS

Seminar 1: Facets of Grace...7

 What is Grace to You?...13

 Sermon: Grace & Justification...25

Seminar 2: Morning Joy...31

 Experiencing Real Joy...47

 The Gift of Joy...50

 Sermon: Freeing Joy in a Prison Cell.............................51

 Sermon: Fulfilling Joy...59

Seminar 3: Authority in Christian Leadership.................70

 Authority and God's Word...78

 Authority and the Local Church.................................85

 Misuse of Authority...88

 Sermon: Authority...90

 Sermon: Real Christians Know When to Bow.............97

Seminar 4: Waiting – There is an Appointed Time.........105

 Characteristics of Waiting: Pre-test.........................107

 How to Wait...115

 Characteristics of Waiting: Post-test.......................117

 Sermon: Patient Waiting...119

Bibliography...127

About the Author...129

OUR RED SEAS

THE RED SEAS OF LIFE

©2014 Brenda Simuel Jackson

Red, a color meaning stop, danger is near. A red sea is a danger that must be crossed, in order to grasp the future without fear.

The red seas of life are many; some are gentle ripples, some raging waves that bury us in caves.

The gentle seas, our first love lost, we went across with godly hope learning that life is not what is lost.

As life progresses, the rage of seas grows taller and taller, job disappearing, health failing, it becomes difficult to ride out the waves.

The wave of cancer drags you under; sin may take your rudder, and you begin to drown; as the wave of abuse smacks you, and you no longer fight but you go down.

The red seas cannot be conquered by individual might; we need divine intervention to simply part them, and rescue us from our plight.

Danger zones can only be crossed with faith in the One Who changes what seems impossible to the gentle calm waters that only He can create.

I see my red seas as possibilities and opportunities to learn to see how much my Lord loves me.

All can share in these possibilities.

FACETS OF GRACE

Grace, a gift from God of unmerited favor.

Grace, a gift from God Who provided salvation.

Grace, a prayer to God expecting deliverance from danger.

Grace, an act of God giving us His mercy.

Grace resulted in our transformation.

Grace provides security which is not of our making.

Grace is security, available for the taking.

Through grace there is life eternally.

Through grace there is holiness and humility.

Through Grace we are servants of God, serving one another.

Grace is the love we give to our Christian sisters and brothers.

Grace in the flesh, and the Spirit is like a jewel; a treasure given to us.

A jewel we must let shine and glow and not collect dust.

FACETS OF GRACE

1 Peter 1:1 – 5:13

GIFT FROM GOD

Study Scripture: Ephesians 2:8

"For by grace you have been saved through faith and that not of yourselves; it is the gift from God;"

Seminar Question: What is Grace?

I.   O.T. roots of grace

    A.   Grace is an action:

        1.   Is not an adverb describing action,

        2.   Compassion from a source able to help another,

        3.   Grace is recognition of transgressions present,

        4.   Psalm 51:1 "Have mercy upon me O God, according to Your lovingkindness, According to the multitude of Your tender mercies…"

[Footnote: Said differently: Have mercy according to your Grace.]

    B.   In O.T. a Hebrew word for grace portrayed as compassion

        1.   Grace – Favor

        2.   Grace – Favor someone

        3.   Grace – What is pleasant

        4.   Grace – What is agreeable

C. Response to the agreeable:

D. Ruth 2:10 finding favor to love – "Why have I found favor in your eyes, that you should take notice of me, since I am a foreigner."

II. N.T. Grace - process of salvation

A. Saved from the wrath of God – Grace
B. Saved despite being guilty – Grace
C. Grace (Youngblood, Ronald, Gen. Ed., 1995) releases favor or kindness shown without regard to worth or merit of the one who receives it and in spite of what that person deserves (552)
D. Grace releases one from bondage (Richards, Lawrence O, 1991).
    1. One is no longer under law – Romans 6:14 – means one is no longer under the law that simply shows the amount of sin
    2. Dominion of Sin – Romans 6:14 – "For sin shall not have dominion over you, for you are not under law but under grace."
E. Grace, a proclamation – An announcement that God in Christ acted and comes to rescue those who trust in Him.
    1. An announcement of how people are trapped in sin
    2. Announcement how one is incapable of pleasing God
F. The Greek term:
    1. Gracious favor bestowed
    2. Causes feelings of gratitude – Romans 6:17; Luke 17:9
    3. Universal
    4. Free in contrast to being in debt
G. Salvation- A gift of Grace – Romans 4:4 NKJV – "Now to him who works, the wages are not counted as grace but as debt."
H. Grace – a gift from God received through repentance and faith

Mini Evaluation of Your Grace

Bondage	Yes	No
Grace freed me from Sex sins?		
Grace freed me from Attitude sins?		
Grace freed me from Pride sins?		
Grace freed me from Envy Sins?		
Grace freed me from Drug sins?		
Grace freed me from Abuse sins?		
Grace freed me from Anger sins?		

III.   God – the source of grace

    A. God's blessing through Christ to those deserving His curse

    B. Common grace

        1. Favor given all men

        2. God causes sun to rise on the evil and the good – common grace (Matthew 5:45)

        3. God is longsuffering – patience for all

            a. Leads one to repent

            b. Withholds His judgment

        4. Common grace – power of Satan is limited

            a. Job 1:12

b. Good and evil benefit

C. Effective grace – Ephesians 2:8 NIV – "For it is by grace you have been saved through faith–and this not from yourselves, it is the gift of God—"

    1. Elements of effective grace

        a. One is dead in sin and follows the world

        b. God's love:

            (1) God rich in mercy

            (2) Made alive in Christ

            (3) Grace saved when we dead in our sins

        c. Grace – God's gift

    2. Called by God – Romans 1:6-7 – "And you also are among those who are called to belong to Jesus Christ"

        a. To all in Rome who are loved by God and called to be saints

        b. Grace and peace to you from God, our Father, and from the Lord Jesus Christ

        c. Grace teaches – God's attitude toward us

            (1) Love

            (2) Acceptance

        d. Grace brings atonement (being made one with God)

            (1) Atonement through Jesus

            (2) Grace through Jesus meets our need of forgiveness

            (3) Grace through Jesus gives us new life

e. Grace cost Christ His death on the Cross – cost man nothing

    (1) Grace requires belief – Acts 16:31 NIV – "Believe in the Lord, Jesus and you will be saved."

    (2) Grace received through God's Word – Romans 10:17 NIV – "…faith comes from hearing the message and the message is heard through the Word of Christ."

    (3) All one has to do for grace is believe – John 3:36 NIV – "Whoever believes in the Son has eternal life, but whoever rejects the Son will not see life, for God's wrath remains on him."

    (4) Grace draws – John 6:44 NIV – "No one can come to Me unless the Father who sent Me draws him…"

IV. Jesus the embodiment of God's Grace (Luke 2:40; John 1:14), brought salvation to mankind

    A. Jesus brought the gospel of Grace into the world

    B. The Grace of God revealed in Jesus

    C. The Holy Spirit applies grace to our lives to live in spiritual wisdom (2 Cor. 1:12)

    D. Grace through the blood of Jesus – establishes the relationship of Christ and the Church

WHAT IS GRACE TO YOU?

(Describe your Gift of Grace)

1st Peter and Grace

Background:

I.   Context

     A.   Hostile Environment (Radmacher, et al. New Illustrated Bible Commentary)

          1.   Hostility to the Gospel

          2.   Christians were targets of pagan religious practices

          3.   Christians were blamed for all things wrong

               a.   Natural disasters

               b.   Economic downturns

          4.   Driven from various cities

          5.   Persecutions

               a.   Slander

               b.   Social ostracism

               c.   Mob riots

               d.   Local police actions

     B.   Imperial ban on Christianity

          1. Issue: Christians refused to sacrifice to the emperor

      2. Herod Agrippa – executing church leaders
        a. First victim was James
        b. Sought to execute Peter [Peter was delivered]

C.   Little Security

    1.   Low social status

    2.   Some were slaves

    3.   Little government protection

D.   Geographic location is Asia Minor (Present day Turkey)

[Describe any similar contexts around the world today which have the same variables as those of the period referenced in 1 Peter]

II.   Key themes in 1 Peter

    A. Encouragement for Christians under stress
    B. Christians can expect to suffer
    C. God uses suffering to shape godly character
    D. Truth of the Gospel.

Broad outline of 1 Peter: (Barker, General Editor, 1985, 1885)

I.   Salutation (1:1-2)

II.   Praise to God for His Grace and salvation (1:3-12)

III.   Exhortations to holiness of life (1:13 – 5:11)

    A. The requirement of holiness (1:13 – 2:3)
    B. The position of believers (2:4-8)
      1. A spiritual house (2-8)
      2. A Chosen people (2:9-10)
      3. Aliens and strangers (2:11-12)
    C. Submission to authority (2:13-3:7)
      1. Submission to rulers (2:13-17)

2. Submission to masters (2:18-20)
3. Christ's example of submission (2:21-25)
4. Submission of wives to husbands (3:1-6)
5. The corresponding duty of husbands (3:7)
D. Duties of all (3:8-17)
E. Christ's example (3:18-4:6)
F. Conduct in view of the end of all things (4:7-11)
G. Conduct of those who suffer for Christ (4:12-19)
H. Conduct of elders (5:1-4)
I. Conduct of young men (5:5-11)

IV.   The purpose of the letter (5:12)

V.   Closing greeting (5:13-14)

Scriptural Overview: [Study these scriptures]

I.   Appearances of Grace in the scriptures

A.   1 Peter 1:2 – The blessings of grace – "Grace and peace be yours in abundance"

B.   1 Peter 1:10 – Grace of expectation – "Concerning this salvation, the prophets, who spoke of the grace [Jesus] that was to come to you."

C.   1 Peter 1:13 – revelation of grace – "Therefore, prepare your minds for action, be self controlled, set your hope fully on the grace to be given you when Jesus Christ is revealed."

D.   1 Peter 4:10 – administering God's grace – "Each one should use whatever gift he has received to serve others, faithfully administering God's grace in its various forms."

E.   1 Peter 5:5 – humility of grace – "Young men in the same way be submissive to those who are older, all of you, clothe yourselves with humility toward one another, because God opposes the proud but gives grace to the humble."

II. Facets of Grace in 1 Peter

    A. Trilogy pattern – three related concepts related to the Throne of Grace

        1. Helping grace comes from the throne of grace

        2. Right for mercy comes from the Throne of Grace

        3. The foundation of salvation is God's mercy (1 Peter 1:3)

    B. Grace in the Old Testament (Richards, Encyclopedia of Bible Words, 1991, p 317)

        1. God's gracious mercy – Psalm 51:1 – "Have mercy on me, O God, according to your unfailing love; according to your great compassion blot out my transgressions."

        2. O.T. represents God's love

        3. Psalms describes God's love (grace) as a source we can cry to for deliverance from foes and circumstances (Richards, 1991)

        4. There is not a direct parallel of meaning of grace in O.T. and N.T.

            a. Grace is Jesus Christ in His humanity

            b. Grace – receiving favor without regard to one's worth of merit to receive

            c. Release from dominion of sin

            d. Believer is under grace

            e. Dispensation (age) of grace ends in judgment

            f. Now in age of the Church and the Holy Spirit

C. In N.T. the theological meaning of grace changes

    1. God aids the undeserving

    2. God aids the helpless sinner

    3. Grace transforms, along with delivering

    4. In Acts, grace is the presence of early Church

    5. Grace gives relationship with God

        a. Through Grace a sinner can be righteous

        b. Through Grace there is redemption

        c. Through Grace is salvation (Romans 3:23-26, 5:15-21, 11:1-10)

    6. The person and work of Jesus Christ is revelation of God's Grace

    7. Through Grace there is life (Ephesians 2:1-10)

    8. Grace is a causative factor

        a. God's love causes God to meet our needs

        b. Grace is conditional

            (1) To receive grace one must trust in God's mercy

            (2) Must trust God's favor (Romans 4:16; Galatian 2:16)

D. The doctrine of security is an aspect of grace

    1. Depends on what God has done

2. When saved, the Holy Spirit places the believer in the body of Christ (1 Cor. 12:13)

3. Holy Spirit seals believers until day of redemption (Ephesians 1:13; 4:30)

4. It is the Father's purpose to keep us (John 10:28-30)

5. Romans 8:29-39 convinces of security (Ryrie, Survey of Bible Doctrine, p. 77-80).

"Praise be to the God and Father of our Lord Jesus Christ. In His great mercy He has given us new birth into a living hope through the resurrection of Jesus Christ from the dead."

1 Peter 1:3 NIV

E. Security in grace – 1 Peter 1:3-11

1. God's provisions

a. Provided for in this life

b. Provides for our future life

c. Shielded by God's power until Christ returns

d. Trials of life refine our faith

e. Future is salvation of our souls

2. The results of Grace

a. God's provisions for now and the future gives power to handle pressures of this life

b. Can maintain joy

c. Can face situations

3. Security is in the Word of God – 1 Peter 1:23-25 NIV

"For you have been born again, not of perishable seed, but of imperishable, through the living and enduring word of God…the word of the Lord stands forever. And this is the word that was preached to you."

4. Because we have a living hope, we have security – 1 Peter 1:3

    a. God gives believer new spiritual life

    b. The Spiritual life enables us to live in a different dimension

    c. Hope – we look toward eternity

5. God's power protects and gives security – 1 Peter 1:4-5

6. Testing our faith gives glory to our Lord – 1 Peter 1:6-7

F. Grace is holiness

    1. Three reasons we should be Holy

        a. God is Holy

        b. God sees our inner attitudes, He judges

        c. Redeemed by the Blood of Jesus

    2. Holiness – divine imitation

        a. Inclusionary process

        b. God invites us to participate in His Holiness

        c. God's gracious sanctification (salvation) is free

        d. Personal holiness

            (1) Self-sacrifice

            (2) Personal discipline

        e. Christ is coming did not change God's expectation of His people – 1 Peter 1:16

        f. The Church is holy

            (1) God consecrated the church

            (2) God's grace sanctifies

    g. Being holy is to be set apart to God

    h. God's eyes are too pure to look on evil with favor – Habakkuk 1:13

    i. Believers should strive for purity

3. "Our heavenly Father is our earthly Judge" (Radmacher et al)

    a. Judged by our deeds

    b. There is no reprieve

    c. God is a merciful Savior

    d. God is our judge

4. Grace and Love as Holiness – 1 Peter 1:22-25

    a. Show holiness by loving others from the heart

            (1) Sincere Love – Romans 12:9

            (2) Hate evil

            (3) Keep the good

    b. John 13:34-35 – New Command to Love one another

    c. Born again

            (1) Dead to sin

            (2) New life in Spirit – Ephesians 2:1

            (3) Washed through regeneration – Titus 3:5

            (4) Perishable becomes imperishable

5. Believers challenged to live holy

a. Challenged to serve God

b. Challenged because our time on earth is short – 1 Peter 1:13-17

c. Although facing evils, Christians are to live righteously

d. Challenged not to return to evil (Radmacher, 1999)

e. God's Grace of redemption produces holiness

f. Through grace live a life dedicated to God – 1 Peter 1:15

g. Grace causes responses to God's holiness

    (1) Leave evil desires

    (2) Adopt God's behavior

    (3) Do not pattern life after fleshly desires

    (4) Obedience to God's will

h. Use mental or spiritually sound judgment. (1 Peter 1:13)

G. Grace serves – 1 Peter 1:16

   1. All our actions are to be submitted to God

   2. Servants of God

   3. Showing proper respect for everyone – All persons are in the image of God

   4. Love demonstrates grace to believers

   5. Workers are to take responsibility seriously

   6. The believer serves the Lord

7. The believer meets the needs of fellow believers (Richards, 551)

8. Grace provides good stewardship

    a. 1 Peter 3:15 NIV – "But your hearts set apart Christ as Lord. Always be prepared to give an answer to everyone who asks you to give the reason for the hope that you have."

    b. Be ready with your testimony

    c. Live according to God's will – 1 Peter 4:4,5

    d. Be administers of God's grace – use your gifts to assist others – 1 Peter 4:10

H. Grace is submission – 2 Peter 2:13-15

    1. "Submit yourselves for the Lord's sake to every authority instituted among men: whether to the king, as the supreme authority, or to governors, who are sent by Him to punish those who do wrong and to commend those who do right. For it is God's will that by doing good you should silence the ignorant talk of foolish men."

    2. Submit to others for the sake of God

    3. Doing right is being true to God

    4. Submit voluntarily to governing authorities

    5. One's submissiveness must line up with the word of God

    6. Do service not grudgingly

7. Do service not with compulsion

8. Service is done with joy

9. Service is done willingly

10. God is glorified

11. Civil disobedience doesn't glorify God

12. Submissive relationship is based on grace

    a. Mutual submissive

    b. Christ willingly submitted

13. Submission is not inferiority

    a. Demonstrates personal significance is not dependent on position

    b. Demonstrates confident submission (Luke 2:51)

    c. Yield to one another out of love (1 Peter 5:5)

14. "Christians are to submit to one another out of reverence for Christ." – Ephesians 5:21 NIV

Scriptures: Romans 3:22-26

Conversation Points:

- The only genuine justice is that received through grace.

- Justification is an act of God.

- Justification required the life of Jesus Christ

Scripture (NIV)

3:22   This righteousness from God comes through faith in Jesus Christ to all who believe. There is no difference,

3:23   for all have sinned and fall short of the glory of God,

3:24   and are justified freely by His grace through the redemption that came by Christ Jesus.

3:25   God presented Him as a sacrifice of atonement, through faith in His blood. He did this to demonstrate His justice, because in His forbearance He had left the sins committed beforehand unpunished–

3:26   He did it to demonstrate His justice at the present time, so as to be just and the One who justifies those who have faith in Jesus.

Book of Romans:

I.   Describes the gospel of salvation in Christ

A. Book is addressed to Saints

    1. Mixed group of Jews and Gentiles

    2. Gentiles – majority of audience

B. Purpose

    1. Provide truth regarding salvation

    2. Provide truths about Christian Living

II. The Book can be divided into five S's (Wiersbe, 1989):

A. Sin – righteousness demanded
B. Salvation – righteousness declared
C. Sanctification – righteousness defended
D. Sovereignty – righteousness declined
E. Service – righteousness demonstrated

[Emphasis is on salvation- Salvation requires Grace and Justification.]

Sermon Discussion:

I. Man needs justification

A. The fall of man (Adam's sin) causes man's need for justification

    1. All have sinned (through being from the seed of Adam)

    2. No difference between sinners

    3. Man keeps falling short

        a. A continuous action (Greek tense)

        b. Cannot measure up to godly standards (Walvoord, 458)

        c.   Cannot achieve righteousness (Radmacher, 1429)

        d.   No one lives perfect, holy righteous life

        e.   There is none righteous

        f.   No one declared righteous

    4.   The law points to the need of justification

II.   Justification is:

    A. Greek term in Epistles, Romans and Galatians

        1. To acquit

           a. To payoff

           b. To repay

           c. To discharge from obligation

        2. To vindicate

           a. Set Free

           b. Deliver

        3. Exonerate

           a. Disposed to

           b. Seek revenge

           c. Provide justification

           d. Protect from attack

           e. Maintain a right

        4. Pronounce righteous

Have you been justified?   Yes   No   I don't know

    B. A legal declaration of righteousness, due to God's action

1. Christ's righteousness imputed to a believer
2. Provided through Grace
3. Appropriated through faith

C. Experiential – God works through Holy Spirit making the believer righteous

D. Being justified – result of believing in Christ as Savior

Have you been justified?   Yes   No   I don't know

E. Justification – a legal act
1. Act of God declaring believing sinner righteous in Christ
2. Edict based on "finished" work of Christ on the cross
3. Legal act valid because Jesus paid the debt of sin
   a. Jesus had no sin
   b. Jesus lived the perfect life
4. Two facets of Romans 3:22-23
   a. Negative view – person declared not guilty
   b. Positive view – person declared righteous
5. Being in right standing
6. Man's righteousness is result of justification – received through faith
7. Person with faith in Jesus Christ stands acquitted now
   a. Acquitted from every charge brought
   b. Acquitted from every future charge

III. Justification and Grace

A. Continuous action

1. All who believe are continuously declared righteous

    a. Declared – make clear

    b. Declared – make known

    c. Declared – make evident

    d. Declared – affirmed

2. Grace provided by God

    a. Freely given

    b. Not something deserved

B. God is just because He is Holy

   1. Perfect righteousness fulfilled in Christ

   2. Christ is justifier of all, our Redeemer

   3. Righteousness of Christ is credited to us

      a. Demands of God's law fulfilled in death of Christ

      b. Experience righteousness of Christ (Romans 3:25-30)

         (1) Justification is grace

         (2) Justification is faith

         (3) Justification results in works

   4. The death of Christ demonstrates God's justice

C. Nothing can erase the righteousness of Christ from our records

MORNING JOY

Experiencing Inner Joy Regardless

Seminar Objectives:

- Understand the distinction between inner joy and outward happiness
- Understand what causes genuine joy
- Learn how to experience true joy regardless of the circumstances
- Learn how to encourage self

MORNING JOY

©2008 Brenda Simuel Jackson

To wake in the morning brings joy.

To move with or without pain sings joy.

To remember Him who gave life twice is the focus of my joy.

To forget past failures and falls, in His forgiveness is the foundation of my joy.

The heaven remains, the earth still is, reasons for joy.

Birds sing, grass dies, souls return to dust, the spirit lives on, reasons for joy.

Love received and given in sickness or in health is joy.

Contentment in good times and in bad times is joy.

When all else fails, He is ever near, and His presence felt, what joy!

I am mindful, weeping may endure for a night, but joy comes in the morning!

What joy is this!

SCRIPTURES	ROOT MEANING	CONTEXT OF THE MEANING
Esther 8:16-17	Hebrew: Gladness Joy Mirth Rejoice In New Revised Standard, joy is a noun meaning without fear.	Jews had joy because the effort to commit genocide against them was changed. They became the victors and the ones to be feared.
Ezra 6:15-16	Hebrew: Joy	The Jews completed rebuilding the Temple. The Jews celebrated the dedication with joy. This dedication is "Hanukah," a Jewish holiday. It is a return to worship.
Job 8:18-21	Hebrew: Delight in the cause or the feeling.	The argument of Bildad to Job that the blameless have (possess) joy.

SCRIPTURES	ROOT MEANING	CONTEXT OF THE MEANING
Psalm 21:1	Hebrew: From the root "to brighten up" Cheer up Be glad Have joy To rejoice	A Psalm of David of his joy in the victories given him by God.
Psalm 27:6	Hebrew: From the root clamor, battle cry, acclamation of joy Trumpet Jubilee Loud noise Rejoicing shout	The people praise because God has given the King victories. The people's praise follows that of the King.

SCRIPTURES	ROOT MEANING	CONTEXT OF THE MEANING
Psalm 42:4	From the root meaning to emit a shrill creaking sound A loud joy A cry out Be joyful Proclamation Rejoicing Shouting Sing Triumph	A prayer of deliverance from oppression. The Sons of Korah (Levite choir) remember how they used to go to the house of God.
Psalm 43:4	Hebrew: A revelation of time of joy Exceeding gladness Rejoicing	A prayer of deliverance from the enemy. Describes the Altar of God as "my joy"…"my delight", words of praise for future action.

SCRIPTURES	ROOT MEANING	CONTEXT OF THE MEANING
Isaiah 65:14	From the root, to be good, goodly, a noun Goodness Beauty Gladness	Judgment of the Lord in the face of refusal of His salvation. Those who accept Salvation will sing from joy in their heart in contrast to those who refuse and will experience anguish in their heart.
Matthew 2:9-10	From the Greek term calmly happy or well off God's speed Joy	The Magi had seen a star in the east. The star stopped over where the child was. They were overjoyed.
Luke 1:44	From the Greek term exultation Welcome Gladness Joy	Mary tells Elizabeth of her expectancy. Elizabeth tells Mary she is blessed and favored because of the Child she bears. Elizabeth explains how the baby leaped for joy when Mary greeted Elizabeth. The object of joy, the Baby in Mary.

SCRIPTURES	ROOT MEANING	CONTEXT OF THE MEANING
John 17:13	The Greek term well, good Mind Feelings of sensitive nature	Jesus' prayer for His disciples, that even in persecution they will have His [Jesus'] joy.
Romans 5:11	The Greek term to vaunt in a good or bad sense Make boast Joy Glory Rejoice	The result of justification causes one to rejoice in God because one is reconciled back to God through Jesus Christ.
Philippians 2:17	Greek Root To be cheerful Calmly happy or well off A salutation on meeting	Paul explains humility, how God worked in the believer and how they sacrifice themselves. Paul rejoices because of their faith.

SCRIPTURES	ROOT MEANING	CONTEXT OF THE MEANING
Philemon 7	Greek term Charis Gracious manner or act Spiritual, divine influence on the heart and reflects in one's life: Acceptable Benefit Favour Gift Joy	The love of Philemon gives Paul joy, encourages the heart, the place of emotions of pity and love.
Philemon 17-20	Greek term to derive pleasure or advantage from Have joy	Translates benefit in letter to Philemon on behalf of fellow prisoner. Paul seeks forgiveness and reconciliation for one who has wronged Philemon, Onesimus. Paul says refresh my heart.

SCRIPTURES	ROOT MEANING	CONTEXT OF THE MEANING
1 Peter 4:13	From the Greek root to jump for joy With Exceeding joy Rejoice greatly	Living for God says one may suffer as Christ suffered. If so, rejoice in that you reveal His glory.

Old Testament meaning of joy:

4. Sense of jubiliation
5. Public exultation (Richards, 1991)
6. Rooted in God
7. God acts for His people (Ibid, 1991)

New Testament meaning of joy:

1. Inner feeling of pleasure
2. Sense of well-being (Ibid)
3. Joy is independent of circumstances (NIV, Richards, Encyclopedia of Words, 1991)
4. True joy, a religious experience

Self Assessment of Your Joy

1. When do you find it difficult to express your joy?

2. Do you separate your joy from happiness?

3. How do you express true joy? Happiness?

4. During difficult times can you feel joyful?

   If yes, why?

   If no, why not?

5. How do you define joy?

6. Can you teach someone to be joyful?

   If yes, how?

7. What is your favorite Scripture involving joy?

Sample Scriptures – (NKJV)

Psalm 30:5b – "Weeping may endure for a night, but joy comes in the morning."

Psalm 51:12a – "Restore unto me the joy of your salvation."

Luke 2:10b – "I bring you good tidings of great joy…"

John 15:11b – "…that my joy might remain…and your joy…"

John 16:22b – "Rejoice and your joy no man takes from you."

Romans 15:13a – "…the God of Hope fill you with joy…"

Jude 24b – "…is able to present you faultless… with exceeding joy."

Focus of and Causes of Joy

I.   Focus and Cause of Joy – (NIV)

    A.   O.T. God's characteristics, His acts cause joy (rejoicing)

        1.   Joy is dependent on God's goodness

        2.   Joy is found in personal relationship with the Lord

            a. Ps. 16:11 – "You have made known to me the path of life; you will fill me with joy in Your Presence, with eternal pleasures at your right hand.

            b. Ps. 19:8 – "The precepts of the Lord are right, giving joy to the heart."

        3.   Joy focuses on God.

a. God's righteousness

    (1) Joy is seen in hope, a proclamation

    (2) Ps. 71:14-16 "…I will always have hope; …tell of your righteousness …I will proclaim your righteousness…."

b. Salvation

    (1) Ps. 21:1 – "O Lord, the King rejoices in Your strength. How great is his joy in the victories You give."

    (2) Ps. 71:23 – "My lips will shout for joy when I sing praise to you – I, whom You have redeemed."

c. Mercy – Ps. 31:7 "I will be glad and rejoice in Your love, for You saw my affliction and knew the anguish of my soul."

d. Creation

    (1) Joy in the praise of God's works.

    (2) Ps. 148:5 – "Let them praise the name of the Lord for He commanded and they were created."

e. Word

    (1) Ps. 119:14 – "I rejoice following your statues as one rejoices in great riches."

    (2) Ps. 119:162 – "I rejoice in Your promise like one who finds great spoil."

    (3) Ps. 33:4 – "For the word of the Lord is right and true; He is faithful in all He does."

B. O.T. characteristics of joy found in God's people

1. Joy is holy

2. Joy is pure

3. Joy rises above circumstances (Youngblood, 1995)

4. Joy is rooted in God

5. Happiness is rooted in things

C. O.T. response in times of trouble

    1. Believer finds joy in expectation that God will deliver

    2. Ps. 33:20-21

        a. We wait in hope for the Lord;

        b. He is our help and our shield

        c. In Him our hearts rejoice"

D. N.T. joy is from the saving relationship with God

E. N.T. joy is from a continuing fellowship with God

F. Joy of a righteous person

    1. God will work things for our good (Romans 8:28)

    2. Joy is becoming more Christ like (Youngblood, 1995)

    3. Joy looks to God

    4. Joy looks beyond present to future salvation

        a. Romans 5:2 – "…through whom we have gained access by faith into this grace in which we now stand, And we rejoice in the hope of the glory of God."

        b. Romans' 8:18 – "I consider that our present sufferings are not worth comparing with the glory that will be revealed in us."

c. 1 Peter 1:4-6 – "and into an inheritance that can never perish…In this you greatly rejoice, though now for a little while you may have to suffer grief..."

G. N.T. joy often linked with persecution (John 17:13,15)

   1. "I am coming to you now, but I say these things while I am still in the world, so that they may have the full measure of my joy."

   2. "My prayer is not that you take them out of the world but that You protect them from the evil one."

   3. Christians' joy is an outcome of salvation

      a. Acts 16:34 – "The jailer brought them into his house and set a meal before them from the evil."

      b. The saving work of God within us provides inexpressible joy

      c. 2 Corinthians 6:10 – "everything is in Christ "sorrowful, yet always rejoicing; poor, yet making many rich; having nothing, and yet possessing everything."

      d. 2 Corinthians 7:4 Description of Paul's joy – "I have great confidence in you…I am greatly encouraged; in all troubles, my joy knows no bounds."

I.   Experiencing real joy

   A.   Outward expression

      2.   The wicked experience a form of joy

         a.   Rev. 11:10 – the inhabitants of the earth is in reference to the unsaved

         b.   The inhabitants celebrate the death of the two prophets

         c.   Express joy by sending gifts

      3.   O.T. joy is expressed by public worship (Richards, 1990)

      4.   O.T. joy is a religious experience

         a.   Believing community gathers

         b.   Praising God is in unison (Youngblood, 1995)

      4.   Receiving God's reward is an experience of joy

         a.   Results from obedience

         b.   Expressed as a celebration of Feast of Tabernacles (Ibid, 1995)

      5.   Joy is shared experiences with other believers

         a.   Sharing in worship

         b.   Sharing in expressing emotions

            (1)   Glad shouts

    (2) Dancing

    (3) Singing songs (Youngblood, 1995)

  6. Joy is experienced as a result of God's actions

   a. Harvest

   b. Military victories

   c. God's faithfulness (Ibid, 1995)

B. Inner Joy

  1. Every human being is hungry for joy (Richards, 1990)

  2. Continual Joy

   a. Memory of God's saving acts (Ibid, 1990)

   b. God's word brings joy

    (1) Ps. 19:8 NIV – "The precepts of the Lord are right giving joy to the heart."

    (2) Ps. 119:14 NIV – "I rejoice in following Your statutes as one rejoices in great riches."

  3. Early missionaries were persecuted

   a. Glowing with joy

   b. Having inner joy

   c. Appearing to deny the circumstances

   d. Acts 13:50, 52 – "But the Jews…stirred up persecution against Paul and Barnabas…and the disciples were filled with joy and with the Holy Spirit.

4. Joy because of confidence in God

    a. Inner sense of exultation

    b. Holy Spirit works in the believer (Richards, 1990)

5. Joy from being obedient to Christ's commands:

    a. John 15:10-11 NIV – "If you obey my commands, you will remain in my love, just as I have obeyed my Father's commands and remain in His love. I have told you that so My joy may be in you and that your joy may be complete."

    b. John 16:24 NIV – "Until now you have not asked for anything in my name. Ask and you will receive, and your joy will be complete."

6. Inexpressible joy – fills the believer

7. Glorious joy fills the believer (1 Peter 1:6-9)

8. Supernatural joy

    a. Joy wells up in painful circumstances (Richards, 1990)

    b. Joy results from obedience

    c. Joy looks to the future

9. Joy is service to fellow Christians

    a. Pride in someone is joy

    b. Romans 16:19 NIV – "Everyone has heard of your obedience, so I am full of joy over you…"

c. II Timothy 1:4 NIV – "Recalling your tears, I long to see you, so that I may be filled with joy…"

d. 1 John 1:4 NIV – "We write this to make our joy complete.

10. Levels of joy

a. Gladness

b. Contentment

c. Cheerfulness

II.   The gift of joy

    A.   Joy is from the Holy Spirit

        1. Romans 14:17 – "For the kingdom of God is not a matter of eating and drinking, but of righteousness, peace and joy in the Holy Spirit."

        2. Galatians 5:17 – "Sinful nature desires what is contrary to the Spirit."

        3. 1 Thessalonians 1:6 – "You became imitators of us… you welcomed the message with the joy given by the Holy Spirit."

    B.   Joy is inner work of the Holy Spirit

        1. Despite trials

        2. Despite suffering

        3. Achieving salvation

    C.   Joy is in God's promises Ps. 119:162 – "I rejoice in your promise like one who finds great spoil."

    D.   Relationship with Jesus is source of joy (John 15:10-11; 16:24)

Conclusion:

Tracing the concept of joy through the Bible helps us realize that our happiness, like our hope, is founded on realities that are unaffected by conditions in this world.

Freeing Joy in a Prison Cell

Sermon

Scriptures: Acts 16:20-28

Conversation: Physical bondage cannot bind the internal Spirit. Those in Christ are free through joy.

Text (Amplified)

16:20 And when they had brought them before the magistrates, they declared, these fellows are Jews and they are throwing our city into great confusion.

16:21 They encourage the practice of customs which it is unlawful for us Romans to accept or observe!

16:22 The crowd [also] joined in the attack upon them, and the rulers tore the clothes off of them and commanded that they be beaten with rods.

16:23 And when they had struck them with many blows, they threw them into prison, charging the jailer to keep them safely.

16:24 He, having received [so strictly] a charge, put them into the inner prison (the dungeon) and fastened their feet in the stocks.

16:25 But about midnight, as Paul and Silas were praying and singing hymns of praise to God, and the [other] prisoners were listening to them.

16:26 Suddenly there was a great earthquake, so that the very foundations of the prison were shaken; and at once all the doors were opened and everyone's shackles were unfastened.

16:27 When the jailer, startled out of his sleep, saw that the prison doors were open, he drew his sword and was on the point of killing himself, because he supposed that the prisoners had escaped.

16:28   But Paul shouted, Do not harm yourself, for we are all here!

Background:

I.   The Book of Acts of the Apostles

    A.   The author – Luke [Luke-Acts]

    B.   The book is a bridge

        1. The life of Jesus

        2. Ministry of the Apostles particularly Paul

    C.   An historical book of the New Testament

        1. Development of Church

        2. Models of Christian Behavior (Harris, 2006)

        3. Models of Christian Service

        4. Fulfillment of O.T prophecies

        5. The New Way (Christianity) for salvation

        6. Results of Power of the Holy Spirit

    D.   Demonstrates that Christianity is not a political tool

    E.   Audience

        1. Gentiles
        2. Converted Jews

    F.   Primary Apostles are Peter and Paul (Harris, 2006)

        1. Peter represents Palestinian Jewish Christianity

        2. Peter represents original Jerusalem Church

3. Peter – first half of Acts (1-12)

4. Paul, the Hellenistic Christian

5. Paul – mission to the Gentiles

6. Paul – second half of Acts (13-26)

7. One third of Acts devoted to Paul's imprisonments

   a. No obstacle can stop God's Word

   b. Song of Miriam – delivery of Israel – no obstacle

   c. Song of Moses – no obstacle

II. The importance of Music and Songs

   A. New Testament used for comfort

   B. Used for worship

   C. On captivity "Songs of Zion" demanded from the captive, by the captors (Ps. 137)

   D. Music in O.T used in making war

   E. Music in O.T used in crowning Kings

   F. Music to celebrate heroes and victories (Webster, 1966)

   G. Music in praise

Conversation:

I. Charges against Paul and Silas and course of events

   A. Proselytizing Roman citizens not permitted

   B. Permitted to have own religion

C.   There was no investigation

        1. Flogged

        2. Imprisoned

D.   Did not go against Roman custom or laws

E.   Those seeking to stop the truth were unscrupulous

F.   False claims made against Jesus

G.   Not the first time Paul beaten for the gospel

H.   Paul did not appeal to his rights as a Roman citizen, as in Jerusalem

        1. Willing to suffer

        2. Knowing a greater work to be done through his imprisonment

I.   Paul and Silas put in maximum security

        1. Inner cell

        2. Fastened feet in stocks

        3. Probably no light

        4. Place used for torture

II.   Singing in midst of suffering:

      A.   (Spirit-Filled Bible) "...Men who sing while they suffer are men who have learned the profound secret that suffering perfects joy,

B. Men who sing in prison are men who cannot be imprisoned."

C. Although chained in stocks, prisoners not imprisoned
1. Fellowship with God
2. Bodily in prison
3. Spiritually with God

D. Those who sing when work stops – never stop working

E. A person who can sing in prison has two objectives
1. Work is never done
2. Never stop witnessing for Jesus Christ

III. Suffering without complaining

A. Philippians 2:14-16
1. Do all things without grumbling
2. Do all things without fault finding.
3. Do all things without complaining against God
4. Do all things without doubting God.

[Why?]

5. Show yourself blameless
6. Show yourself guiltless
7. Show that you are in the middle of crookedness
8. But, you are the light

B. The other prisoners saw Paul and Silas, lights in the middle of darkness

[To whom are you a light?]

1. The darkest hour
2. Paul and Silas praying and singing
   a. In the inner prison
   b. In maximum security
   c. A time of joy
   d. Psalm 42:8 AMP – "Yet the Lord will command His loving-kindness in the daytime, and in the night His song shall be with me, a prayer to the God of my life."
3. In times of darkness, the light of a Christian witness shines brightest
   (Radmacher, 1999)
4. The listening prisoners
   a. Listened with perception
   b. Listened with pleasure
   c. Listened to beautiful music

[Witnessing is music to somebody's heart. (Radmacher, 1400)]

C. The results of pure joy
   1. Doors opened
   2. Earthquake forced door posts apart, locks holding the doors closed fell off
   3. Jailer frightened
      a. Thought prisoners escaped

b. All were there

c. Jailer saved – experienced joy of salvation

d. Free from physical and spiritual death (Jailer)

Scriptures: Philippians 2:1-5, 14-18

Conversation: True unity in the Church is a result of having a Christ-like attitude of humility. There is joy in being like Christ. An attitude of humility is an attitude of service.

Scriptures (NIV)

2:1   If you have any encouragement from being united with Christ, if any comfort from His love, if any fellowship with the Spirit, if any tenderness and compassion,

2:2   then make my joy complete by being like-minded, having the same love, being one in Spirit and purpose.

2:3   Do nothing out of selfish ambition or vain conceit, but in humility consider others better than yourselves.

2:4   Each of you should look not only to your own interests, but also to the interests of others.

2:5   Your attitude should be the same as that of Christ Jesus:

2:14   Do everything without complaining or arguing,

2:15   so that you may become blameless and pure, children of God without fault in a crooked and depraved generation, in which you shine like stars in the universe

2:16   as you hold out the word of life – in order that I may boast on the day of Christ that I did not run or labor for nothing.

2:17   But even if I am being poured out like a drink offering on the sacrifice and service coming from your faith, I am glad and rejoice with all of you.

2:18   So you too should be glad and rejoice with me.

Background (Philippians 1:3-29):

I.   Author – Paul

    A.   Epistle written from prison

        1. House arrest in Rome

        2. Two years in prison

    B.   Evangelized the gospel

    C.   Church at Philippi established on 2nd missionary journey of Paul

        1. 1st convert – Lydia

        2. Found Lydia and other women worshipping outside the city on riverbank

    D.   A missionary progress thank you letter

        1. Thanks for gift received during detention

        2. Thanks for reports of his circumstances

        3. Encouragement to stand in face of persecution

        4. Rejoice regardless of circumstances

        5. Giving commendations

        6. Warning against false teachers

    E.   Shares secrets of "lasting joy and inner peace." (Youngblood, 785)

    F.   Encourages full commitment to Jesus (Ibid)

II.   Theological Concepts:

A.   Hymn of Praise to Jesus
     1.   Avoid rivalry
     2.   Cultivate humility (Harris, 492)
         a.   Ancient world despised humility
         b.   Christians see humility as a virtue
         c.   Model Jesus' behavior
         d.   Surrender completely to God's will (Ibid)

B.   Theme of fulfilling the joy of Jesus

     1.   Fulfill – to put into effect

         a.   To bring to an end

         b.   To measure up to

         c.   To satisfy

         d.   To develop full potentialities

         e.   To perform

     2.   In Philippians, joy and rejoice when combined mentioned seventeen times in one form or another

         a.   Joy, a noun

         b.   Rejoice, a verb

         c.   Joyous, an adjective

         d.   Rejoice, having a reason for joy

         e.   Happy is not a noun, but an adjective.

            (1)   Favored by luck or fortune
            (2)   Fortunate
            (3)   Well adapted
            (4)   Pleasant
         d.   Biblical use of happy

         (1)   Condition of wellbeing

         (2)   A result of being blessed (Youngblood, 468)

3.   Joy in O.T

    a.   Sense of exultation rooted in God

    b.   Exultation through God's acts for His people

    c.   Expressed through public worship (Ibid, 589)

4.   Joy in the N.T.

    a.   Inner sense of exultation in God.

    b.   Inner sense of confidence in God which is worked through the Holy Spirit in life of Believer

    d.   Through Holy Spirit will experience joy despite suffering (Ibid)

5.   What activates our joy

    a.   Confidence in God, Ps. 16:11 – "You have made known to me the path of life; you will fill me with joy in your presence...."

    b.   [Those who received the good news], gladness over the birth of Jesus – Matthew 2:10

    c.   Joy over future rewards in heaven – Luke 6:23; 10:20

    d.   Joy in knowing that the bridegroom, Jesus Christ is coming – John 3:29

    e.   Worthy of suffering disgrace for His Name – Acts 5:41

    f.   Joy in hope – Romans 12:12

       g.   Joy in accomplishments of others – Acts 16:19

       h.   Joy in truth – 1 Corinthians 13:6

       i.   Joy in visits of others – Acts 16:17

       j.   Joy in suffering (Colossian 1:24) – "Now I rejoice in what was suffered for you…."

6.   Occasions that bring rejoicing

       a.   His incarnation – Philippians 3:1; 4:4

       b.   His power – Luke 1:14

       c.   His presence with the Father – Luke 13:14

       d.   Being with Jesus – John 16:22

       e.   Rejoice on hearing the gospel – Acts 13:48

       f.   Rejoice at our salvation as did the Eunuch who was baptized by Philip – Acts 8:36-39

       g.   Rejoice having liberty in Christ – Acts 15:31

       h.   Rejoice in fellowship – Philippians 2:28

       i.   Rejoice in your faith – Philippians 1:25

[God is the object of our joy.]

Conversation:

I.   Initiating fulfilling our joy in Christ Jesus

    A.   Encouraged because we are united in Christ

       1. Our personal union in Christ is reality of our salvation

2. Reality of being rescued from sin

3. Reality of being rescued

4. Real joy

B. Encouraged through benefits of our relationship with Christ – Joy

1. Joy because of His comfort

2. Joy because of His love

3. Joy because of fellowship among believers produced by the Spirit within

4. Joy because of compassion and care for one another

5. Benefits of unity

   a. Encouragement

   b. Comfort

   c. Fellowship

   d. Compassion

II. Being united in Christ helps us to follow His path of humility and obedience

A. Humility – surrendering to the will of the Father

1. Humility is not weakness

2. Humility is rejection of selfishness – that is fulfilling joy

3. Humility is active concern for the interest of others – That is fulfilling joy in Christ Jesus

4. Like-minded, one in Spirit and purpose – that fulfills the joy

5. An attitude of Christ

   a.   Working together – fulfills joy

   b.   Serving each other – fulfills joy

6. There is joy in spiritual unity

   a.   Rejoice for like-mindedness

   b.   Rejoice for the same love

   c.   Rejoice as we are one in Spirit

   d.   Rejoice as we are one in purpose

   e.   Maintaining proper attitude toward self fulfills joy

   f.   Seeing others as worthy of preferential treatment fulfills joy

   g.   Self-sacrificing humility and love for others fulfills joy

7. Self-centeredness does not bring true joy

   a.   Paul says do nothing out of selfish ambition

   b.   Humility puts others before self

   c.   Pre-occupation with oneself is sin, it is prideful

   d.   Enemy of unity – selfish ambition

   e.   Enemy of unity – vain conceit

[In facing our problems – we fulfill the joy in Christ Jesus.]

III. In confronting problems, God works in us to do His will

    A. We are enabled to do the will of God
    B. We are working out our salvation

        1. Work out solutions for today's issues

        2. Following the example of Jesus is doing the will of God

        3. We do His will without complaining

        4. We do His will without arguing

    C. Fulfilling the joy is shining like stars

        1. Being light in dark places

        2. Being discontent with God's will is expressing unbelief

        3. Discontent is a barrier to doing what pleases God – 1 Corinthians 10:10

        4. Characteristics of joy fulfilled

            a. Not debating unimportant issues – joy fulfilled

            b. Blameless – joy fulfilled

            c. Pure and holy – joy fulfilled

            d. Devoted to doing God's will – joy fulfilled

        5. We live in a crooked and depraved time (unbelievers)

[therefore]

            a. We must shine

            b. Our lives should effectively turn away unrighteous accusations

            c. Fulfilling the joy of Jesus, being blameless, not perfect but above reproach

            d. We look depravity in the face and shine like stars

e. Our witness is out of love

f. The light of the gospel is seen in our lives

g. Our defense is what God has done through our lives (Rejoice)

h. We can rejoice about the Day of Christ's return, saying we stood with Christ

   (1) You stood for the best

   (2) You stood for the Word of life

   (3) We stand because we will be saved although what we preach is foolish to some

   (4) We stand for our spirit will be saved although the sinful nature will be destroyed

   (5) Rejoice – yet holding on to faith in Christ

II. We rejoice and do not sorrow

A. Paul's life was a sacrifice – yet he rejoiced.

1. He rejoiced for the Philippians

2. He rejoiced to God

3. His death was near, yet he rejoiced

4. His life was an act of worship

5. The work of the Philippians was an act of worship

B. Is our life, a true worship service

1. Can we rejoice in Him who was our sacrifice?

2. Can we rejoice in Him who set us free?

3. Can we rejoice in Him who intercedes for us now?

4. Can we rejoice in our eternal life, a gift from Him?

C. Let us fulfill our joy in Christ Jesus through our worship of Him

AUTHORITY

©2010 Brenda Simuel Jackson

I have authority because I have the freedom to choose.

I have authority, if used correctly, I cannot lose.

The authority given to me is to serve and to help others to be free.

To serve is the best way to lead, for then you can really see.

See Jesus, the true leader, and a suffering servant was He.

The church has a head to whom all should bow, the Divine Shepherd, and

His chosen under shepherds are the leaders to follow.

Exercise your authority by submitting your will to the One and Only
Authority Who is genuine and real.

SEMINAR OBJECTIVES

- Understand what is Christian Authority
- Understand Authority in the Church
- Understand Authority of the Word
- Understand Obedience and Authority
- Understand Rebellion and Authority

Authority Self Assessment

1. Who had authority in your home/living arrangement when you were between the ages of 0 - 5 years of age?

    _____

2. Did you obey rules when you were between ages of 5 – 10 years of age?

    Yes ___   No ___

    Why?

    _____

    Why Not?

    _____

3. Who had authority in your High School class room?

    _____

4. Did you obey classroom rules? Yes ___ No ___

5. Have you ever purposely run a red light? Yes ___ No ___

6. Have you purposely driven a vehicle on an expired license? Yes ___ No ___

7. On your first job, who had authority?

    _____.

8. Did you respect the person or the authority of the person?

    The Person Yes ___ No ___   The Authority Yes ___ No ___

9. Is Jesus Lord of your life? Yes ___ No ___

10. If answer 9 is yes, answer questions 11 and 12, if no go to question 13

11. Do you obey the commands of Jesus such as love your enemy? Yes ___ No ___

12. Who has authority over your daily living?
    _____

13. Describe the authority you have in your life:

14. Is your authority from the Lord or from man? The Lord ___ Man ___

15. In exercising your authority, who is glorified?
    _____

Foundational Scriptures for the Seminar

Romans 13:1-7 (NIV)

13:1   Everyone must submit himself to the governing authorities, for there is no authority except that which God has established. The authorities that exist have been established by God.

13:2   Consequently, he who rebels against the authority is rebelling against what God has instituted, and those who do so will bring judgment on themselves.

13:3   For rulers hold no terror for those who do right, but for those who do wrong. Do you want to be free from fear of the one in authority? Then do what is right and he will commend you.

13:4   For he is God's servant to do you good. But if you do wrong, be afraid, for he does not bear the sword for nothing. He is God's servant, an agent of wrath to bring punishment on the wrongdoer.

13:5   Therefore, it is necessary to submit to the authorities, not only because of possible punishment but also because of conscience.

13:6   This is also why you pay taxes, for the authorities are God's servants, who give their full time to governing.

13:7   Give everyone what you owe him: If you owe taxes pay taxes; if revenue, then revenue; if respect, then respect; if honor, then honor.

I.   Authority – Definition (Vines, 45)

    A.   Power of one whose will and commands must be obeyed by others

1.   Spiritual power – Matthew 9:6; 21:23; 2 Corinthians 10:8

2.   Power of rule

3.   Power of government

4.   Liberty (Exousia)

5.   Ability given

6.   Strength given

B.   Hearing which brings understanding and obedience (Richards, 331)

1.   Obedience, an attitude – 2 Corinthians 2:9; Philippians 2:12

2.   Obedience in Christ is faith.

3.   Expression of a heart turned to God (Richards, 462)

4.   Response to what is heard (Youngblood, 908)

II.   Types of authority (Richards, 91-95)

A.   Secular – Human government
B.   Power to Control
    1.   Legal control
    2.   Political control
    3.   Social control
    4.   Moral control

C.   Supernatural control (Richards, 87)

1.   Supernatural beings

2.   Influences human events

D.   Elders

      1.   Local assembly leaders

      2.   Spiritual guides

Romans 13:

I.   Authority and Secular governments in scriptures:

A.   God permits secular governments

B.   God provides principles as guides in hostile territory

      1.   Impact of Christian living in secular environment

            a.   Tension between the divine, the spiritual and the secular

            b.   Commitment to live quiet lives

            c.   Manner of living that mitigates tensions

[How did you respond to government's handling of issues of abortion? Same sex marriages?]

      2.   Unjust government

            a.   Choose to do what is right

            b.   Accept suffering for doing what is right – 1 Peter 3:13-14

      3.   Dual Citizenship

            a.   Exercise citizen rights

               (1)   Legal rights

    (2) Political activity

    (3) Influence law making (Richards, 91)

   b. Responsibilities (Romans 13)

    (1) Paying taxes

    (2) Acting with respect

    (3) Praying for all persons – 1 Timothy
2:1-2

    (4) Following the laws

 D. Human government revealed by God

  1. God put one human in rule over another – Genesis
3:16

  2. At end of time, human government destroyed –
Revelation 18

  3. Human governmental institutions began in the
beginning – Genesis 9:5-6)

   a. Man held accountable for life of fellowman.

   b. Death penalty instituted

   c. No government and authority = chaos –
Genesis 4:19-24

II. Authority and obedience

 A. Adam's disobedience to God's Authority

  1. Disobedience brought physical death

  2. Disobedience broke the relationship with God.

 B. Christ's obedience to God's authority – Romans 5:12-21

1.   Grace

2.   Righteousness

3.   Life

4.   Christ – Principle of Obedience (Nee, 46-47)

       a.   Gave up personal authority

       b.   Submitted to Father's authority – John 14:28

C.   God's authority maintained through obedience (Nee, 53-59)

1.   God's will

2.   God's sovereignty

III.   Authority and Disobedience

A.   Midwives disobeyed local authority to obey a higher authority

B.   The three Hebrew Youths disobeyed local authority to obey a higher authority

C.   Daniel disobeyed local authority to obey a higher authority

D.   Peter in preaching disobeyed local authority to obey a higher authority

Are you obeying a higher authority?

I. The Bible – What it is

    A. Holy written record of the Word of God

        1. Mark 12:26 – "But concerning the dead being raised – have you not read in the book of Moses…how God said to him…(cross reference Exodus 3:2-6)

        2. Luke 20:42 (Amplified) – "For David himself says in [the] Book of Psalms, The Lord said to my Lord…."

    B. The word Bible is from the Greek word, Biblos, biblos, book

        1. References the Old Testament, Hebrew Bible:

            a. Torah for Law

            b. Prophets

            c. The Writing

        2. O.T in Hebrew and Aramaic Languages

    C. The Bible, a record of promises, covenants of God in Old and New Testaments

        1. Genesis 12:1-3 – "The Lord said to Abram…I will make you into a great nation and I will bless you; I will make your name great, and you will be a blessing…all peoples on earth will be blessed through you."

2.   Luke 22:20 and 1 Corinthians 11:25 – "This cup is the new covenant in My Blood, which is poured out for you..." (God's saving grace)

3.   Hebrew 9:15 – "...receive the promised eternal inheritance...free from sins committed under the first covenant."

II.   Divine origin of the Bible – Authority of the Bible

     A.   The Bible is from God

         1.   2 Timothy 3:16-17 – "All scripture is God-breathed and is useful for teaching, rebuking, correcting and training in righteousness..."

         2.   God-breathed – God actively involved in writing Scriptures

         3.   2 Peter 1:20-21 – "...no prophecy of Scriptures came about by the prophets' own interpretation...but men spoke from God as they were carried along by the Holy Spirit."

         4.   2 Peter 3:15-16 – "...Paul...wrote you with the wisdom that God gave him. He writes the same way in all his letters..."

         5.   Exodus 14:1 NLT – Moses writes "and spoke Jehovah to Moses saying..."

         6.   Over 2000 times in most versions of O.T., writers affirm, "This is what the Lord says" or "The Word of the Lord came to..."

         7.   The Apostles testify their writings were God's commandments

             a.   1 Corinthians 14:37 (Paul) – "If anyone thinks he is a prophet or spiritually gifted let him acknowledge that what I am writing to you is the Lord's command."

             b.   2 Peter 1:16-18 – "We did not follow cleverly invented stories... We ourselves heard this voice that came from heaven when we were with him on the sacred mountain."

8. The Bible is testimony of Holy Spirit – 2 Peter 1:19-21

B. For believers in Jesus Christ, faith provides testimony of divine authorship of the Bible
   1. Jesus accepted every word
   2. Jesus quoted the words
   3. Jesus used the word to rebuke evil
   4. Matthew 4:4 refers to Deuteronomy 8:4 – "Jesus answered, 'It is written Man does not live on bread alone, but on every word that comes from the mouth of God.'"

C. The Bible divinely developed
   1. Unity of the 66+ books
   2. 66+ books had 40 writers, with 40 different backgrounds, who wrote about one God
   3. Written with unity over a 1500 year span
   4. 66+ individual books make one Book
   5. Divine origin seen in the indestructibility of the Bible
   6. The Bible has historicity
      a. Bible is verifiable
      b. Archaeological finds verify events, times, places
         (1) Hezekiah's tunnel
         (2) Solomon's stables
         (3) Jericho's walls
         (4) Jesus' birth place

         (5) Jail of Paul and Silas

      c. Speaks to historical reliability

      d. Does not prove or disprove religious statements

      e. Reveals fulfilled prophecies

f.   Provides symbolic acts not mythical things

D.   God's Inspiration

    1.   Word inspiration in Greek means inspired by God.

        a.   Qeo – (Theo) God and rneuma – (pneuma) To breathe is translated revelations and inspiration (Greek-English Lexicon)

        b.   God's inspiration caused the writing

        c.   God's inspiration caused revelation or personal encounter with God (Ryrie, 65-66)

    2.   Statements of noted theologians

        a.   Charles C. Ryrie, 65-66 – "Inspiration is oversight of God and His relationships with writers ranged from very direct i.e. Moses to less so i.e. Paul."

        b.   Enns, 156 – "inspiration is Holy Spirit's superintendence over the writers so that while writing according to own style and personalities the results was God's work."

        c.   Warfield – "Supernatural influence bring divine trustworthiness."

        d.   Young – "Superintendence of Holy Spirit results in divine authority, trustworthiness and freedom from error."

III.   The Bible is inerrant, without error or fault

    A.   Inerrant in absolute truth

        1.   Truth in doctrine

2.   Truth in teachings

3.   Truth in circumstances

4.   Truth in situations

5.   Truth in happenings

B.   Scripture passages which present difficulties for inerrancy resolved

      1.   Sound analytical processes

      2.   Utilizing original language

      3.   Harmonizing (Example: The reports of Judas' death can be harmonized through Acts 1:18; Matthew 27:5-9)

      4.   Conjecture

IV.   The Bible as Canon is the Bible as Authority

A.   Canon means rule, the Bible is a rule book
B.   Canonicity is quality of the rule
C.   Fact that books from God gives canonicity
D.   Tests of inclusion – Tests of canonicity
      1.   Divine authorship
      2.   God speaking through a mediator
      3.   Human author a prophet or spokesperson of God
      4.   Historically accurate
      5.   Reflects actual facts.
      6.   Book received by the Jewish people
E.   Dead Sea Scrolls is evidence of authenticity of Old Testament
F.   Non-canonical references substantiates the inclusion of Books into the Canon (Jude)
G.   Church fathers affirmed 39 books of Old Testament
H.   New Testament testifies of the Old Testament

     I.   New Testament is affirmed
          1.   The authors had been with Christ
          2.   Letters read in Churches and circulated
          3.   New Testament events (crucifixion) found in history

VII.   Authority is the preached and the taught Word

     A.   O.T – teach the law from generation to generation – Deuteronomy 4:9
     B.   Psalm 19 praises God's Law
         1.   It communicates God's will
         2.   Provides enlightenment
         3.   Causes wisdom
         4.   Causes rejoicing
     C.   Leads to a fruitful life
     D.   Leads to abundant life through fellowship with God (Harris, Archer, & Waltke, 405)
     E.   God is the teacher
         1.   Exodus 4:15 – Who is the teacher? Who is the student?[1]
         2.   Psalm 25:8 – Who is the teacher? Who are the students?[2]
         3.   Psalm 25:12 – What causes learning?[3]
         4.   Exodus 18:10 – Who is the teacher?[4]
     F.   Jesus taught His disciples from the Bible
         1.   Romans 2:20 – "you then have in the law, the embodiment of knowledge and truth."
         2.   Ephesians 4:11 – The Lord appointed persons to have gift to teach

---

[1] God is the teacher and Moses is the student
[2] God is the teacher and sinners are the students
[3] The fear of the Lord causes learning. See Deuteronomy 4:10, 14:23; 17:19; 31:12,13
[4] Moses is the teacher, and possible students are judges.

I.   Scriptures define two offices within the local church

   A.   Overseer or bishop – 1 Timothy 3:1

       1.   Sixteen (16) qualifications to be met by those who seek to fill this office – 1 Timothy 3:1-7

       2.   Overseer is elder of Church

           a.   Elder provides administrative leadership – 1 Timothy 5:1-17
           b.   Elder pastors the members – 1 Peter 5:2
           c.   Elders instruct the church – 1 Timothy 3:2b
           d.   Elders pray on behalf of the members – James 5:14-15

   B.   Office of Deacon (1 Timothy 3:8-13; Act 6:1-3)

II.   Authority (according to Scripture) of the local church

   A.   Operates by the power of the Holy Spirit
   B.   Exists by power of the Holy Spirit
   C.   Exists to carry out the Lord's will
   D.   The church divinely established
   E.   Continues the Lord's presence on earth
   F.   Is to be pure
   G.   Discipline
       1.   Corrective action for an errant brother or sister
       2.   Restoration of believer back to righteous behavior – Matthew 18:15
       3.   Remove that which tarnishes the whole church – 1 Corinthians 5:7

I.   Adam and Eve

    A.   Adam abdicated his given authority position when followed Eve

    B.   Adam and Eve disobeyed God's Authority

    C.   No authority higher than God

II.   Korah and 250 leaders in congregation opposed Moses with words – Numbers 16

    A.   Korah and his followers were chastised for going against Moses

    B.   Cannot go against the Lord's anointed

III.   Miriam and Aaron spoke against Moses.

    A.   Arrogance
        1.   Challenged God's anointed – Numbers 17:10-12
        2.   Levites vs. Priests, Leaders going against Aaron – Numbers 17

    B.   Strange Fire

        1.   Nadab and Abihu – Leviticus 10:1-2

        2.   Offered sacrifice without approval of God

        3.   Form of rebellion against authority

IV.   Noah rebelled against authority in his sin

    A.   Drunken condition
    B.   Uncovering of his nakedness[5]

---

[5] His nakedness may have indicated sexual emission in his drunkenness.

V.   Satan rebelled – pride goes against authority – Ezekiel 28:13-19

VI.   The Lord judges those who rebel against authority

      I.   Korah judged (he was killed)
      II.   250 Leaders judged (they died)
      III.   Miriam judged (she suffered with leprosy)
      IV.   Those who went against Aaron were killed
            1.   The Lord chose Aaron
            2.   The censors of the non-chosen were taken
      V.   Nadab and Abihu killed immediately
      VI.   Noah seen by his sons
      VII.   Satan and his angels thrown from heaven and eternally condemned

VII.   Cannot accept God and reject His delegated authority (Nee, 116-121)

      A.   Rebelling against God's chosen is sin against God
      B.   Spiritual work requires cooperation not individual effort

I.   Personal Thoughts – making decision on personal thoughts not God's Direction

    A.   Moses misrepresented God – Numbers 20:2-3, 7-13

        1.   Demonstrated lack of faith

        2.   Demonstrated the wrong spirit

        3.   Spoke wrongly

    B.   Eli not chastising his sons for misusing their priestly office – 1 Samuel 3:11-13

Christian Authority

I.   Jesus Christ gives authority

    A.   Builds the believer

    B.   Submits to authority

        1.   Yield to governance

        2.   Commit to judgment of another

        3.   Yield to another's will.

    C.   Submit to one another

II. Christian Authority – Submission

    A. Submit self to governing authorities (Richards, 584)
    B. Surrender personal interest – Romans 12:10; Philippians 2:3,4
    C. Freely subordinates self to someone
    D. Choose to obey
    E. Situational submission
        1. Voluntary choice
        2. Following cultural norms
    F. Submission is not being inferior; it is obedience to God

AUTHORITY

Background Scriptures: Matthew 16, 18; Acts 5:3, 9

Discussion Scriptures: Matthew 16:16-19; Matthew 18: 15-18

Argument: The believer's authority cannot go beyond the rules already promulgated in heaven.

Scriptures (NIV)

Matthew 16:18-19

16:18 And I tell you that you are Peter, and on this rock I will build my church, and the gates of Hades will not overcome it.

16:19 I will give you the keys of the Kingdom of heaven; whatever you bind on earth will be bound in heaven, and whatever you loose on earth will be loosed in heaven.

Matthew 19: 15, 18

19:15 If your brother sins against you, go and show him his fault, just between the two of you. If he does not listen take one or two others along... If he refuses to listen to them, tell it to the church; and if he refuses to listen, to the church,...treat him as you would a pagan or a tax collector.

19:18 I tell you the truth, whatever you bind on earth will be bound in heaven, and whatever you loose on earth will be loosed in heaven.

I.   Key words in these passages

    A.   Keys – a means of control (Webster, 1966)

1. Something that gives a solution

2. Something that provides an explanation

3. An object that locks and unlocks

4. Keys are a source of binding and loosing

5. Keys are to the Kingdom of Heaven – Matthew 16:19

B. Binding and Loosing

   1. Bind (Webster, 1966)

      a. Make secure by tying

      b. To confine, restrain

      c. To put under obligation

      d. To constrain with legal authority

      e. Restrained freedom

   2. Loose (Webster, 1966)

      a. Release

      b. Free from restraint

      c. To detach

      d. Make less rigid

   3. Loose (Vines, 379)

      a. Dismiss

      b. Forgive

        c.   Release

    4.   Rabbinic literature stated what was prohibited and what was permitted

    5.   Tense implies what is loosed or bound on earth will have been determined already in heaven

    6.   Promise of divine direction for each local church (Radmacher, 1174)

    7.   The power to bind and loose is the authority to expel persons from the congregation

    8.   The power to receive persons back into the congregation. (Richards, 126)

C.   Authority

    1.   Keys of the kingdom, binding and loosing keys, serve as badge of authority (Kaiser, 385)

        a.   Rabbinical Judaism

            (1)   Denotes promulgation of rulings to forbid various activities

            (2)   Promulgation of rulings authorizing various activities

        b.   Keys Peter received to bind and loose

        c.   Keys disciples used to bind and to loose

    2.   Old Testament Concept

        a.   Responsibility

        b.   Care

   c. Superiority

   d. Dominion

   e. Power

   f. Scriptures: Genesis 16:9, Judges 9:29; 2 Chronicles 23:18; 31:13,15; Jeremiah 38:10-11; Isaiah 19:4; Proverbs 16:32 (Richards, 92)

  3. New Testament concept (Richards, 92)

   a. Authority can be divine or human

   b. Used wisely or foolishly

   c. Used to benefit or to exploit others

   d. Can be given or forced

   e. Accepted or Rejected

  4. "God ordained authorities to restrain sin." (92)

  5. Exousia – Greek term for authority

   a. Basic concept is freedom of choice

   b. Greater the exousia the greater possibility of unrestricted freedom of action

II. Authority in the Future Kingdom and Church discipline

 A. Two aspects (views) of binding and loosing

  1. 1st view – Peter given authority to make binding decisions

2. 2nd view – Peter chosen to open the door of the Gospel to two major groups

    a. Pentecost

    b. 1st gospel message preached (Richards, 567)

3. Peter is promised divine guidance in making decisions.

6. Peter has authority in the Kingdom – loosing and binding

    a. Affirm forgiveness of sin and retention

    b. We speak God's Word of Authority not our own

    c. Christ shared His Authority with His disciples (Richards 567)

7. The Apostle by ministry of the Word of Life keeps unbelievers outside the Kingdom of God

8. The Word admits into the Kingdom those who believe (Vines, 66)

B. Loosing and binding is carrying out God's instructions

C. Authority to bind or loose given disciples – Matthew 18:18 – involves church discipline

1. Peter's rebuke of Ananias was binding

2. Peter's rebuke of Sapphira was binding

3. The binding was ratified in heaven – Acts 5:3, 9

D. Expelling of a person from the Church is not expelling from salvation

1. The act of binding (rules already established in heaven)

2. The actions of binding and loosing directed from heaven (Walvoord, 62)

3. Jesus, Who directs us, acts through us to loose and bind with authority (Richard 567)

III. Freedom of Action

A. The authority to control or limit the freedom of actions of others

1. Authority is derived in the body of Christ

2. Pharisees wanted to know where Jesus got His authority

a. Mark 3:15; 6:7 – Jesus delegated authority to His disciples over demons and diseases

b. 2 Corinthians 13:3 – Paul had authority to choose to discipline wrong doer in the Church

B. A person without exousia has little freedom of action

(Richards)

1. Without exousia (authority), one under the exousia of others.

2. Without exousia others control one's actions

3. Exousia to become God's children given only to those who believe in Christ

4. Ephesians 2:1-2 – Sin limits freedom of action of non-believers

C.   One who rejects correction steps out of fellowship with the Lord

      1.   Matthew 18:18 – If one rejects correction, they step out of fellowship with brethren on earth (Richards, 93)

      2.   Matthew 18:1-35 – When believers repent, forgiveness should be unlimited (vv. 21-22)

D.   Matthew 18:15-20 – Decisions made by the Church will be ratified in heaven

      18:19   Again, I tell you that if two of you on earth agree about anything you ask for, it will be done for you by my Father in heaven.

      18:20   For where two or three come together in my name, there am I with them. **AUTHORITY!**

Real Christians Knows When To Bow

Sermon

A Real Christian Knows How to Bow

Scriptures: Hebrews 13:17, Romans 13:1

Argument: Obedience is the better sacrifice

Submission is the better road to success

Background Scriptures: Titus 3:1; Ephesians 6:5-9; 1 Peter 2:13

Scripture texts: (NIV)

Hebrews 13:17

Obey your leaders and submit to their authority. They keep watch over you as men who must give an account. Obey them so that their work will be a joy, not a burden, for that would be of no advantage to you.

Romans 13:1-2

Everyone must submit himself to the governing authority for there is no authority except that which God has established. The authorities that exist have been established by God.

Consequently, he who rebels against the authorities is rebelling against what God has instituted and those who do so will bring judgment on themselves.

BACKGROUND:

I.   Relationship, a key in the book/epistle of Hebrews

    A.   Relationship between our Lord, and the The Church

    B.   Emphasis is the superiority of Christianity to Judaism.

II.   The Head is the Authority (Relationship to the Church)

    A.   Matthew 28:18 [Jesus Speaks] – "All authority in heaven and on earth has been given to Me."

        1.   Authority – power to be obeyed

        2.   Authority – His commands

        3.   Authority – His Will

    B.   Spiritual "Potentate"

        1.   Makes plain the administration of the Gospel – Ephesians 3:10

        2.   Make known God's revelation through the Church

    C.   Struggle with powers of the dark world relying on God's armor

        1.   Spiritual battle

        2.   Spiritual tools

    D.   Thrones/Powers/Rulers authorities created – Colossians 1:16

        1.   Created by Christ

        2.   Created for Christ

    E.   Christ is head over all powers and authorities – Colossians 2:10-15

F.   Authorities and powers are in submission to Christ who is at right hand of God – 1 Peter 3:22

III.   The Head has the right to exercise power

     A.   Power of rule

     B.   Power of government

     C.   Exousia, Greek term for authority

         1.   Liberty to exercise power (Vines, 45)

         2.   Operate in the strength given.

IV.   Authorities – rules and authorities in all levels of human government

[Transition: Authority indicates a relationship to those over which have authority. Requires obedience and submission (Let us bow). In USA Today, January 22, 2010, the headline states: "Contractor Agrees to remove Bible references." The article states "Michigan defense contractor will voluntarily stop stamping references to Bible verses on combat rifle sights made for the U.S. military, a major buyer of the company's gear…the references to Bible passages raised concern that the citations break a government rule that bars proselytizing by US Troops in Afghanistan and Iraq which are predominantly Muslim countries." Did this rule violate God's commands? Was it appropriate for the contractor to bow to the law? There are voluntary situations of obedient submission to authority. To whom will glory be given?]

V.   When to bow

     A.   Obedience – meaning

1. Personal relation (to our Lord)

2. Motivation (Love of our Lord) [John 14:21 – "Whoever has my commands and obeys them, is one who loves Me," says Christ.]

   a. To obey is to love

   b. To obey is to hear

      (1) To hear is to understand

      (2) To hear is to respond

      (3) To hear is acting in accordance to God's purpose

      (4) To hear says there are no complaints against God's will

      (5) To hear is to have one's heart turned to God

   c. Obedience in Christ is faith; it is an attitude of service

B. Submission is a response to obedience

   6. Submission – surrendering personal interest to those of others (bow down)

   7. Subordinate self to someone (bow down)

   8. Choosing to obey (bow down)

   9. Submitting (bow down)

      a. To lower

      b. To yield to governance or authority

        c.   To commit to judgment of others

        d.   To yield to the will of others

10.   Voluntary submission

        a.   Interpersonal relationships

        b.   Christians submit to one another in reverence to Christ – Ephesians 5:21

11.   Situational submission

        a.   Voluntary choice of believer

        b.   Judgment of what is right according to customs – what are the customs in Federal prison?

C.   Submission is not synonymous to inferior – all are equal in Christ regardless of gifts

6.   Leader Characteristics

        a.   Speaks the Word of God

        b.   Life is a legacy of how to live righteously – Hebrews 13:7

        c.   Recognizes responsibilities of being a shepherd

            (1)   Protects

            (2)   Teaches

            (3)   Disciplines

(4)   Finds the lost

(5)   Provides peace

    d.   Under shepherd commissioned to watch over soul (the life) spirituality of the flock

(1)   Accountable to God

(2)   Accountable at the judgment seat of Christ

  D.   Disobeying is refusing to bow – makes the Shepherd's job harder – Hebrews 13:17

    6.   Show respect

    7.   Show orderliness in the Church

    8.   Let yourself be persuaded

    9.   Not blind obedience

      a.   Obey Christ as Lord

      b.   Not a surrender of personal responsibilities

VI.   Civil government ordained by God

  A.   Civil government – governing authorities (should bow)

    1.   Civil rulers – maybe pagan as during when time of Romans was written (should bow)

    2.   Obedience given as not a violation of low of God (should bow)

    3.   Do what is right in God's sight (should bow)

B.   Disobeying human government is disobeying God (should bow)

    1.   God ordained system – 1 Peter 2:13

    2.   God permitted authority to be established among men

C.   When to bow in civil situations

    1.   Submit to rulers and authorities

    2.   Obey rulers – Romans 13:1-7

    3.   Be ready to do whatever is good – Ephesians 2:10

    4.   Be peaceable in action

    5.   Be considerate in action

    6.   Show true humility

    7.   Attitude of willingness to respond to secular leaders

    8.   Obey the government

    9.   Citizens of heaven who submit to earthly governments promotes well-being in a community

E.   Behavior of submission teaches godly behavior to those in authority – Titus 2:9

F.   Keep the Lord as your focus

VII.   The obedience and submission of Jesus Christ provides salvation to the world

A.   The Will of the Father was done

B.   The authorities who crucified Him came to faith through His behavior

C.   He bowed the lowest that anyone could go, by dying on the cross for us

D.   He is King of Kings

E.   He is Lord of Lords

F.   Every Knee shall bow to Him

G.   Every tongue confess His Lordship

Can we do no less than those He has appointed? Bow Down!

SEMINAR 4

WAITING

There is an Appointed Time

SEMINAR OBJECTIVES:

- To explain the relationship between waiting and hope
- To describe the benefits of waiting
- To describe positive waiting

WAITING FOR THE APPOINTED TIME

It was an appointed time for Mom when I was born.

It was an appointed time for me when from Mom's apron strings I was torn.

It was not a time appointed when from the right way, I strayed. It was not a time appointed when graduation from school was delayed.

It was not a time appointed when drugs became my trade.

It was an appointed time when God, my life He saved!

I have learned, God has an appointed time for a positive plan for me, all I need do is actively wait with hope and glee.

There is an appointed time for God's plan.

I wait with eager expectation, knowing my future is in His Hands.

CHARACTERISTICS OF WAITING:

Pre-Test:

True False

1. It is OK to sleep late when waiting to hear if I got the job.

2. It is appropriate not to send out new resumes while waiting to hear from my last interview.

3. There is no need to send thank you notes after the interview for I claim the job.

4. I am to continue my daily prayers for success in employment while waiting for the job.

5. I can wait because I am confident in myself.

6. I do not grow weak while waiting for change in my future.

7. Twenty-five years is too long to wait!

8. There are benefits in waiting.

9. Redemption is not related to waiting.

10. Christians do not need to wait.

Foundational Scriptures of the Seminar:

Habakkuk 2:3 (NKJV)

For the vision is yet for an appointed time; but at the end it will speak, and it will not lie. Though it tarries, wait for it; because it will surely come, it will not tarry.

Isaiah 40:31 (NKJV)

But those who wait on the Lord shall renew their strength; they shall mount up with wings like eagles, they shall run and not be weary, they shall walk and not faint.

Lamentation 3:22-26 (NIV)

Because of the Lord's great love we are not consumed, for his compassions never fail. They are new every morning; great is Your faithfulness. I say to myself, "The Lord is my portion; therefore I will wait for Him." The Lord is good to those whose hope is in Him, to the one who seeks Him; it is good to wait quietly for the salvation of the Lord.

Conversation

I.   The Lord's great love is why we wait

    A.   Great love in Hebrew is plural

        1.   Stresses God's faithfulness

        2.   Stresses God's commitment to His covenant promises

        3.   Psalm 89:1 – describes how great is God's love

4.   God brings grief, but He shows compassion [Great Love]

5.   God's faithfulness together with His love demonstrates His covenant mercies toward His people [Great Love]

6.   Not every person in Jerusalem was consumed

        a.   Prophet left (he wrote)
        b.   Remnant left (they read what was written)
        c.   [Great Love]
7.   Remnant left because of God's love
8.   Remnant left because of God's mercy
9.   God remembers to be merciful even in His wrath
10.   God's compassion cannot be exhausted (Elwell, 556) [Great Love]

D.   Judah [We] not abandoned by God because of His Loving Kindness
    1.   Cannot measure God's compassion
    2.   Everyday is opportunity to experience God's love
    3.   Jeremiah, in midst of sorrow was seeking God's mercy (Youngblood, 952)
    4.   God's mercy is like manna
        a.   Enough for each day
        b.   New every day
        c.   Can't save, one is to use it

II.   The Lord is my inheritance:

A.   To receive from the Lord, an eternal possession
B.   Legacy of Priest and Levites
    1.   Psalm 73:26 – "My flesh and my heart may fail, but God is the strength of my heart and my portion forever."
    2.   The Psalmist here is a Levite
    3.   Numbers 18:20 – "The Lord said to Aaron, you will have no inheritance in their land, nor will you have

any share among them; I am your share and your Inheritance among the Israelites."

4.   Hope in Him [The Lord], is "expectant confidence", why we can wait, with confident attitude

5.   God brings restoration
       d.   Must wait on Him
       e.   Only God rescues, so we must wait on Him

III.   God is Faithful

     A.   As Jeremiah waited in midst of mistrust of others, we wait
     B.   Those who wait
       1.   Accept God's will
       2.   Accept God's timing
       3.   Hope while waiting

IV.   Hope in God is worth the waiting

     A.   No one with hope in God will be put to shame
     B.   The treacherous will be exposed
     C.   The Lord answers prayers, Psalm 86:7 – "In the day of my trouble, I will call on You, for You will answer me."
     D.   The Lord is good
       1.   Psalm 34:8 – "Taste and see [experience Him] that the Lord is good."
       2.   The man who takes refuge, security in Him, is blessed
       3.   God is good for all people who wait and hope in Him

[I describe this generation as the microwave, instant generation; can they wait in the Lord? Are you part of the microwave generation?]

V.   Waiting

     A.   To remain in readiness (Youngblood, 1297)

     B.   To be in expectation

C.   Confidence that God will act on your behalf

D.   Working out of hope.

E.   Continuing steadfastly – Mark 3:9

F.   To look for with view of favorable reception (Vines, 663)

G.   Expecting eagerly (Romans 8:23)

H.   Hoping – Isaiah 49:23

      1.   (NIV), "…those who hope in Me will not be disappointed."

      2.   (NKJV), "…For they shall not be ashamed who wait for Me."

VI.   Waiting Situations

      A.   Virgins, male and female, wait until after marriage for sexual relations
      B.   Couples wait to marry until can afford to marry
      C.   A spouse waits until mate returns from the battle
      D.   The ill wait for the report
      E.   The unemployed wait for employment
      F.   The pregnant wait to deliver
      G.   The incarcerated wait for parole or release
      H.   The lonely wait for companionship
      I.   The lawless wait for legal action

VII.   Biblical reasons to wait. (Read each accompanying Scripture and apply to your waiting situation.)

      A.   Salvation – Genesis 49:18
            1.   A prayer for help
            2.   Looking for deliverance

      B.   Answered prayer(s) – Psalm 25:1-4

1.   Mercy

2.   Deliverance

3.   Guidance

4.   Pardon

C.   The Holy Spirit – Acts 1:4

D.   The coming of the Messiah

E.   The Kingdom of God – Psalm 37:34; Luke 12:36; 1 Thessalonians 1:10

F.   Redemption – Psalm 130:5-7

G.   Spiritual gifts – 1 Corinthians 12; Ephesians 4:11

H.   Blessings – Proverbs 8:34

I.   Renewed Strength – Isaiah 40:31

J.   Inheritance – Psalm 37:9

K.   Death – Job 14:14

THOSE WHO DID NOT WAIT

SCRIPTURES	CONTEXT	RESULTS
Genesis 16:1-10	Sarai and Abram was given a covenant promise from God. Sarah would bear a son. After years of waiting, Sarai had not conceived, she gave her hand maid, Hagar, as a surrogate. Hagar bore a son, Ishmael.	The first born of Abraham was out of the will of God. A pagan nation resulted. Abraham had to send this son away.
1 Samuel 13:7-14	Saul waiting for Samuel, the Prophet, to offer sacrifice and inquire about the battle that Saul is ready to fight. Saul waited 7 days, and when Samuel did not come, Saul assumed the role of High Priest and Prophet and did his own sacrifice.	Another reason why Saul lost the Kingdom and God's favor.
Exodus 32:1-6	The Israelites had been led out of Egypt by the mighty hand of God, led by Moses to Mount Sinai. Moses went up into the Mountain to communicate with God and to receive God's law for His people. The people tired of waiting, "Now when the people saw that Moses delayed coming down the mountain…the people gathered together. Aaron…make us gods that shall go before us…Moses…we do not know what has become of him."	Sin and judgment: The worse kind of sin against God is idolatry and immorality. God's wrath and judgment resulted and there was the death of thousands.

What happened when you could not wait?

THOSE WHO WAITED

SCRIPTURES	CONTEXT	RESULTS
Genesis 41:37-41	Joseph, sold by his brothers into slavery, was thrown into the palace jail after being falsely accused of attempted rape. He was forgotten for two years by the cup bearer who promised to remember the help he received from Joseph, who interpreted a dream for him. Joseph did not stop doing righteously during his time of waiting for his release.	The cupbearer finally remembered and recommended Joseph to the King to interpret the King's dreams. Salvation resulted as Joseph was used to save God's people.
Luke 2:25-32	Simeon, a devout and just man was waiting for the "Consolation of Israel." He believed the Lord, who told him he would not die until he saw the salvation of the Lord. Simeon was in the temple when Joseph and Mary brought Jesus to the temple for circumcision and dedication.	Simeon recognized Jesus as the Salvation of God. "Lord, now You are letting Your servant depart in peace…For my eyes have seen Your salvation."

Describe the results you received when you waited on the Lord.

VIII. How to Wait

    A.   Have confidence in God's goodness – Psalm 25
          1.   Know God gives delight
          2.   Know God gives favor
          3.   Know God does good when it is not deserved
          4.   Know God's acts are beneficial
    B.   Let your goodness be seen
    C.   Keep following Christ and His Word – Psalm 37:34
    D.   Be prepared for service at all times (in and out of season) – Luke 12:35-36
    E.   Know what and for whom you are waiting
    F.   Be in active service – 1 Thessalonians 1:9-10
    G.   Be honest in your waiting – true hope
    H.   Be righteous in your dealing as you wait – Luke 2:25
    I.   Be devout, reverencing God in your behavior and communications – Luke 2:25
    J.   Examine yourself and your motives while waiting – 1 Corinthians 11:33
    K.   Be respectful of others
    L.   Have courage, take risks – Psalm 27:14
    M.   Study God's plan – Habakkuk 2:3
    N.   Wait quietly, peacefully – Lamentations 3:25-2
          1.   Accept God's will
          2.   Demonstrate confidence in Him
    O.   Stay connected
          1.   Know to Whom you should be connected (the right network)
          2.   Know what relationships to maintain while waiting – 1 Samuel 1:23
    P.   Persevere – Continue
    Q.   In fellowship with others seeking the same goal(s) – Acts 1:4
    R.   In opposition to those who are Anti-Christ
          1.   Those against Kingdom building
          2.   Those seeking to break your focus – Mark 15:43

REFLECTIONS:

1. Describe a specific change or goal for which you are waiting:

2. How long have you been waiting? _____.

3. Describe any negative aspects associated with your waiting:

4. Describe your hope(s), your expectation(s) to result from your waiting:

5. What are you doing as you wait?

6. Where is your trust and confidence as you wait?

CHARACTERISTICS OF WAITING:

Post-Test:

True False

1. It is OK to sleep late when waiting to hear if I got the job.

2. It is appropriate not to send out new resumes while waiting to hear from my last interview.

3. There is no need to send thank you notes after the interview for I claim the job.

4. I am to continue my daily prayers for success in employment while waiting for the job.

5. I can wait because I am confident in myself.

6. I do not grow weak while waiting for change in my future.

7. Twenty-five years is too long to wait!

8. There are benefits in waiting.

9. Redemption is not related to waiting.

10. Christians do not need to wait.

[Note any changes from your pre-seminar responses on test #1.]

SCRIPTURES TO AID THE WAIT

- Isaiah 40:31
- Lamentations 3:19-26
- Psalm 13
- Psalm 23
- Psalm 25:4-5
- Psalm 27
- Psalm 130
- Isaiah 42:1-9

Patient Waiting

Sermon

Scriptures: Isaiah 40:29-31

Romans 12:11-13

Hebrews 12:1-2

Conversation: To wait is to hope with increased faith, and with Christian behavior

Text: NIV

Isaiah   40:29-31

29.   He gives strength to the weary and increases the power of the weak.

30.   Even youths grow tired and weary, and young men stumble and fall;

31.   but those who hope in [wait for] the Lord will renew their strength. They will soar on wings like eagles; they will run and not grow weary, they will walk and not be faint.

Romans 12: 11-13

11.   Never be lacking in zeal, but keep your spiritual fervor, serving the Lord.

12.   Be joyful in hope, patient in affliction, faithful in prayer.

13. Share with God's people who are in need. Practice hospitality.

Hebrews 12:1-2

1. Therefore, since we are surrounded by such a great cloud of witnesses, let us throw off everything that hinders and the sin that so easily entangles, and let us run with perseverance the race marked out for us. [Set Time]

2. Let us fix our eyes on Jesus, the Author and Perfecter of our faith, Who for the joy set before Him endured the cross, scorning its shame and sat down at the right hand of the throne of God.

Background

I. Patience is a reaction to circumstances

    A. Determines how one waits

    B. Reaction to troubles

    C. Reaction to emergencies

    D. Recognizes God's sovereignty

    E. Recognizes the responsibility of being a Christian

    F. Teaches us how to wait

II. The Book of Isaiah

    A. Book of comfort

    B. Written 150 years before Cyrus, Persian King was used to bring salvation to Judah

      1.   Addressed to Babylonian exile – prophecy

      2.   Reader under threat of Assyrian conquest

      3.   Isaiah encourages the people to remember God never relaxes [Helps us in waiting]

C.   Chapters 40-55

      1.   Speaking to Judean captives

      2.   Prophecy of liberation [Wait on the fulfillment]

III.   What is Patience?

A.   An abiding under (Vines, 493)

      1.   Grows in trials (it's only a test)

      2.   Gives endurance

      3.   Provides fruit of the gospel

B.   Perfects Christian character

C.   Challenges the Christian to run the race before them

[With the help of patience, one is able to exhibit confident waiting – knowing the outcome]

IV.   What is waiting (Webster, 1966)

A.   To stay in place in expectation

      1.   No cuts

      2.   No save my place

3.   No getting out of line

B.   To delay in hope of a favorable change

C.   Because of hope, have courage to continue to wait

D.   In Hebrew, to hope is translated wait

E.   Wait confidently until God acts

Exposition:

I.   Affirmation of God's promise

     A.   Isaiah – exile will end [Doing time will end!]

     B.   God sets free [Set Time, Wait on Him]

          1.   People were disheartened

          2.   Asking will God truly establish His Kingdom

          3.   You ask will God set me free

          4.   God's nature

               a.   Salvation

               b.   God's nature – restoration

               c.   God's nature – faithful

               d.   God will strengthen you as you wait for the promise

          5.   God gives strength to the weak

a. Those who hope in the Lord – remain faithful to God

b. Through God you will have the strength of an eagle

c. Prepared to soar

    (1) Golden eagle 8 feet wingspread

    (2) Nest in high inaccessible places

    (3) Can spot his prey while soaring hundreds of feet in air

    (4) Mother eagle carries eagle on her back until masters flying [God will carry you through this]

    (5) Swift in flight

    (6) Belief – eagle renews its strength [youthful appearance after shedding its feathers.]

d. Psalm 103:5 – strength of people nourished by God is like strength of eagle

[Are you strong enough to wait?]

6. The Lord delivered Israelites – He will deliver you, wait on Him

[Exodus 19:4 – "You yourselves have seen what I did to Egypt, and how I carried you on eagles wings and brought you to myself."]

7. In captivity – Israel was weary – you get weary waiting

a. Weary waiting in line

b.   Weary waiting in doctor's office

c.   Weary waiting to file unemployment

d.   Weary waiting in chow line

e.   Weary waiting for parole board

8.   The Lord will help you endure your waiting

a.   Lord will help you soar

b.   Lord will see you are uplifted emotionally

c.   Lord will uplift you spiritually

d.   The Lord gives power to those who trust Him

[Keeping waiting]

e.   To wait –

(1)   Confident expectation

(2)   Active hope in the Lord

(3)   Not passive resignation – hopelessness

[Remember Jeremiah 29:11 "For I know the plans I have for you declares the Lord, 'plans to prosper you and not to harm you, plans to give you hope and a future."] Wait I say, wait!

II.   The people of faith testify to God's Truth

    A.   Must run race with perseverance while waiting

        1.   Stay focused on Jesus, you can wait

        2.   Jesus author, the way to faith

        3.   Divest, remove anything that hampers this spiritual race, self discipline

        4.   Christ has done everything necessary for us to endure

        5.   Christ is our example

            a.   Joy set before Him

            b.   Didn't focus on suffering

            c.   Don't focus on own circumstances

            d.   Will not crumble under difficulties

            e.   Continue your courage and hope

    B.   While Waiting

        1.   Share with God's people

        2.   Practice friendliness/hospitality (encourage someone else)

        3.   Keep an attitude of serving

        4.   Keep your zeal

        5.   Be joyful in hope – keep waiting

        6.   Hope in Christ – keep waiting don't give up hope

7. Be in constant prayer – rejoicing in hope

C. Realized Faith – remember those rewarded for waiting

 1. Abraham waited 25 years – received the blessing, received the promise

 2. Jacob – waited for the promised wife

 3. Joseph, sold into slavery and put in prison, waited two years for freedom and exaltation

 4. Anna, Prophetess, widowed at a young age, waited in the temple until she was 84, but she saw God's Salvation – "then she started looking forward to Jerusalem's redemption." – Luke 2:36-38

6. Simeon was promised he would not die until he saw the Messiah – He did!

7. The one who was an invalid, waited on the movement of water, and for someone to put him in the water for 38 years then came Jesus

Keep waiting – Hope will be realized.

BIBLIOGRAPHY

Bibles

Barker, Kenneth, ed. *NIV Study Bible New International Version*. Grand Rapids, MI: Zondervan, 1985.

Lockman Foundation. *KJV – Amplified Holy Bible, Parallel Bible*. Grand Rapids, MI: Zondervan,1987.

Radmacher, Earl D., Allen, Ronald B., and House, Wayne H, eds. *The Nelson Study Bible, NewKing James Version*. Nashville, TN: Thomas Nelson Publishers, 1997.

Thompson, Frank Charles, ed. and compiler. *The Thompson Chain – Reference Bible*. New American Standard Bible. Indianapolis, IN: B.B. Kirkbride Bible Co.1993.

New Spirit-Filled Life Daily Bible, New King James Version. Nashville, TN: Thomas Nelson, 1993.

Books

Arndt, William F. and Gingrich, F. Wilbur. *A Greek-English Lexicon of The New Testament and Other Early Christian Literature*. Chicago, IL: University of Chicago Press, 1999.

Brown, Francis, Driver, S.R., Briggs, Charles A. *A Hebrew and English Lexicon of The Old Testament*. Oxford, England: University Press.

Elwell, Walter A. ed. *Baker Commentary on the Bible*. Grand Rapids, MI: Baker Books, 1989.

Enns, Paul. *The Moody Handbook of Theology*. Chicago, IL: Moody Press.

Books Cont'd

Harris, Laid R., Archer, Gleason L., and Waltke, Bruce K. eds. *Theological Wordbook of the Old Testament.* Chicago, IL: Moody Press, 1980.

Harris, Stephen L. *Understanding the Bible.* 7th ed. Boston, MA: McGraw Hill, 2006.

Kaiser, Jr, Walter C. et al. *Hard Sayings of the Bible.* Illinois: IVP Academic, 1996.

Nee, Watchman. *Spiritual Authority.* Christians Fellowship Publishers, 1972.

Radmacher, Earl, Allen, Ronald B., and House, H. Wayne. *Nelson's New Illustrated Bible Commentary.* Nashville, TN: Thomas Nelson, 1999.

Richards, Lawrence O. *New International Encyclopedia of Bible Words.* Grand Rapids, MI: Zondervan Publishing House, 1991.

Ryrie, Charles C. *Basic Theology.* USA: Victor Books, 1982.

Ryrie, Charles C. *A Survey of Bible Doctrine.* Chicago, IL: Moody Publishers, 1977.

Vine, W.E., et al. *Vine's Complete Expository Dictionary of Old and New Testament Words.* Nashville, TN: Thomas Nelson Publishers, 1985.

Walvoord, John F. and Zuck, Roy B. eds. *The Bible Knowledge Commentary.* Chariot Victor, 1983.

Webster's Seventh New Collegiate Dictionary. Springfield, MA: G&C Merriam Co.

Youngblood, Ronald F. Gen. Ed. *Nelson's New Illustrated Bible Dictionary.* Nashville, TN: Thomas Nelson, 1995.

ABOUT THE AUTHOR

 Brenda Simuel Jackson (BA, MA, Master of Divinity, Ph.D. Certified Biblical Counselor), is a born again Christian, affiliated with the Baptist Denomination. She is a member and Minister of New Prospect Missionary Baptist Church, and does ministry through BSJ Christian Seminars, Inc., Prison/Jail Ministry. She is a graduate of Wayne State University, and Moody Theological Seminary – Michigan, formerly Michigan Theological Seminary. She has also obtained a second doctorate in Divinity at Jacksonville Theological Seminary with a concentration in prison ministry. She is a member of the pulpit, teaching, and prison ministries of her church.

Dr. Jackson has over thirty years of professional experience in human services, education administration, and management, as well as part-time collegiate instruction. She is currently a part-time faculty member of Wayne County Community College District. She has presented at Conferences of the American Association of Christian Counselors, local church women's retreats, mission programs, Christian Education Institutes, State Correctional Facilities, as well as Professional and Community Programs.

Dr. Jackson is a published writer who released her first book entitled, *A Journey of Redeeming Faith,* in April 2007. It was the first of four seminar compilations entitled, *Reflections on the Path to Wholeness.* The second in the series entitled, *Being Wonderfully Made"* was released April, 2008, and the third in the series, *Going Through"*, was released in October, 2009. *Cross Roads,* the last in this series, was released in April, 2010. In her second series, *The Ongoing Struggle* is three additional books entitled *Cross Roads* (2012), *Freedom in a Cag*e (2014), and now this work, *Red Seas: Overcoming*. Dr. Jackson also hosted a radio broadcast, "God's Teaching Moments." Her Christian Journey includes short term outreach mission and prison ministry assignments in Japan, South Africa, Jamaica, and Ghana. Dr. Jackson completed prison ministry in Zambia, Africa in December, 2011.

A native Detroiter, Dr. Jackson is a widow, a mother, grandmother, great grandmother, and ninth child of Willie and Lucy Simuel (both deceased). Dr. Jackson is a called minister of the Gospel. Dr. Jackson was licensed as a minister of the Gospel November 13, 2005. Having obtained a certification as a Chaplain; in 2013 Dr. Jackson obtained a Doctor of Philosophy in Divinity Degree with a major in prison ministry. Her vineyard is the prisons of the world.

BOOK ORDER FORM

The Ongoing Struggle: Vol 3
Red Seas: Overcoming
Brenda S. Jackson, Ph.D.

Name _____

Address _____

City _____ State _____ Zip _____

Phone _____ Fax _____

Email _____

Quantity	
Price *(each)*	$11.99
Subtotal	
S & H *(each)*	$1.99
MI Tax 6%	
TOTAL	

METHOD OF PAYMENT:

☐ Check or Money Order

(*Make payable to*: **BSJ Christi**

☐ Visa ☐ Master Card ☐ Amer

Acct No. _____

Expiration Date (*mmyy*) _____

Signature _____

Mail your payment with this form to:
BSJ Christian Seminars
P. O. Box 21004
Detroit, MI 48221

BOOK ORDER FORM

The Ongoing Struggle: Vol 2
Freedom in a Cage
Brenda S. Jackson, Ph.D.

Name _____

Address_____

City _____State _____Zip _____

Phone _____Fax _____

Email _____

Quantity	
Price *(each)*	$11.99
Subtotal	
S & H *(each)*	$1.99
MI Tax 6%	
TOTAL	

METHOD OF PAYMENT:

☐Check or Money Order

(*Make payable to*: BSJ Christi

☐Visa ☐Master Card ☐Amer

Acct No. _____

Expiration Date (*mmyy*) _____

Signature _____

Mail your payment with this form to:
BSJ Christian Seminars
P. O. Box 21004
Detroit, MI 48221

BOOK ORDER FORM

The Ongoing Struggle: Vol 1
Cross Roads
Brenda S. Jackson, Ph.D.

Name _____

Address _____

City _____ **State** _____ **Zip** _____

Phone _____ **Fax** _____

Email _____

Quantity	
Price *(each)*	$11.99
Subtotal	
S & H *(each)*	$1.99
MI Tax 6%	
TOTAL	

METHOD OF PAYMENT:

☐ Check or Money Order
(*Make payable to*: **BSJ Christi**

☐ Visa ☐ Master Card ☐ Amer

Acct No. _____ CVV _____

Expiration Date (*mmyy*) _____

Signature _____

Mail your payment with this form to:
BSJ Christian Seminars
P. O. Box 21004
Detroit, MI 48221

BOOK ORDER FORM

Reflections on the Path to Wholeness: Vol 1
A Journey of Redeeming Faith
Brenda S. Jackson, Ph.D.

Name _____

Address _____

City _____ **State** _____ **Zip** _____

Phone _____ **Fax** _____

Email _____

Quantity	
Price *(each)*	$9.99
Subtotal	
S & H *(each)*	$1.99
MI Tax 6%	
TOTAL	

METHOD OF PAYMENT:

☐ Check or Money Order

(*Make payable to*: **BSJ Christian Semina**

☐ Visa ☐ Master Card ☐ American Expre

Acct No. _____ CVV _____

Expiration Date (*mmyy*) _____

Signature _____

Mail your payment with this form to:
BSJ Christian Seminars
P. O. Box 21004
Detroit, MI 48221

BOOK ORDER FORM

Reflections on the Path to Wholeness: Vol 2
Being Wonderfully Made
Brenda S. Jackson, Ph.D.

Name _____

Address _____

City _____ State _____ Zip _____

Phone _____ Fax _____

Email _____

Quantity	
Price *(each)*	$11.99
Subtotal	
S & H *(each)*	$1.99
MI Tax 6%	
TOTAL	

METHOD OF PAYMENT:

☐ Check or Money Order

(*Make payable to*: **BSJ Christian Sem**

☐ Visa ☐ Master Card ☐ American Ex

Acct No. _____

Expiration Date (*mmyy*) _____

Signature _____

Mail your payment with this form to:
BSJ Christian Seminars
P. O. Box 21004
Detroit, MI 48221

BOOK ORDER FORM

Reflections on the Path to Wholeness: Vol 3
Going Through
Brenda S. Jackson, Ph.D.

Name _____

Address _____

City _____ **State** _____ **Zip** _____

Phone _____ **Fax** _____

Email _____

Quantity	
Price *(each)*	$11.99
Subtotal	
S & H *(each)*	$1.99
MI Tax 6%	
TOTAL	

METHOD OF PAYMENT:

☐ Check or Money Order

(*Make payable to*: **BSJ Christian Seminars**)

☐ Visa ☐ Master Card ☐ American Express

Acct No. _____

Expiration Date (*mmyy*) _____

Signature _____

Mail your payment with this form to:
BSJ Christian Seminars
P. O. Box 21004
Detroit, MI 48221

BOOK ORDER FORM

Reflections on the Path to Wholeness: Vol 4
Crossroads
Brenda S. Jackson, Ph.D.

Name _____

Address _____

City _____ State _____ Zip _____

Phone _____ Fax _____

Email _____

Quantity	
Price *(each)*	$11.9 9
Subtotal	
S & H *(each)*	$1.99
MI Tax 6%	
TOTAL	

METHOD OF PAYMENT:

☐ Check or Money Order

(*Make payable to*: **BSJ Christian S**

☐ Visa ☐ Master Card ☐ American

Acct No. _____

Expiration Date (*mmyy*) _____

Signature _____

Mail your payment with this form to:
BSJ Christian Seminars
P. O. Box 21004
Detroit, MI 48221

Lightning Source UK Ltd.
Milton Keynes UK
UKOW06f0925130915

258536UK00012B/179/P